Praise for *The Book of Alice*

"As much a restoration as it is a reimagining, a return of Black women to our rightful place as the center of the world and of the Word. These brilliant, breathtaking poems, brimming with intimacies and interrogations, are at once familial and universal. *The Book of Alice*'s cup runneth over with quiet devastations and resistances, across generations and time. This is a book I'll keep close to my heart."

—Deesha Philyaw, author of *The Secret Lives of Church Ladies*

"Calling *The Book of Alice* one of the best collections of the twenty-first century would be an understatement. I do not know that I have ever read a better book about grandmothers in my readerly life. Diamond Forde handles frequencies, pauses, and traditions like a conjurer of the highest rank. I'm most taken by the sound of the book. This is as ecstatic as literature gets."

—Kiese Laymon, author of *Heavy*

"*The Book of Alice* climbs back through the branches of the family tree, calling down ancestral voices to sing inside poems inspired by biblical tradition, recipes, a census report, and other formal containers. Forde unfurls family secrets and truths across her pages, dancing past the barriers of bloodline-memory to discover what sweetness or sharpness lives on the other side. Most delightfully, Forde's dynamic language gallops through this book, irresistible to read out loud: 'batter / buttered, harpooned with jam . . . & I crop top, too. Coquette / my blubber, my bust.' *The Book of Alice* invites the reader into a kind of wonderful veneration—of the body, of the family, and of the holy self."

—Maria Zoccola, author of *Helen of Troy, 1993*

"A gospel of inheritance in which reckoning, grief, labor, and love converge in a finely wrought hymn. These poems thrum with vernacular holiness and unflinching music under Forde's pen, transforming domestic ritual into divine speech. *The Book of Alice* is both sacred text and living archive, a testament to the mothers who endured and the daughters who refuse to let their rich legacy dim."

—Airea D. Matthews, author of *Bread and Circus*

"Visionary. These poems are as brilliantly made as they are soul stirring, and Forde, using style and craft, explores the past and present. She honors not only her grandmother, Miss Alice, but ours. Writing like this remind us of poetry's propensity to heal. I'm so excited for people to read these poems. They are a balm for our times."

—Crystal Wilkinson, author of *Praisesong for the Kitchen Ghosts*

"Diamond Forde is a cartographer mapping the landscape of survival—a country that every Black woman has had to chart. *The Book of Alice* takes an unflinching look at the life of a beloved matriarch passing down Her gospel. Forde's ambitious use of persona and form allow us to meditate on doubt, betrayal, self-love, and what it means to be your own savior. These poems are as unsparing as they are merciful, as nostalgic as they are mournful, as smart as they are felt. To live is to know you will be introduced to grief, but also love. And that love can be fashioned into a kiss, a recipe, a balm, or a blade."

—Karisma Price, author of *I'm Always So Serious*

THE BOOK OF ALICE

POEMS

DIAMOND FORDE

SCRIBNER
New York Amsterdam/Antwerp London
Toronto Sydney/Melbourne New Delhi

Scribner
An Imprint of Simon & Schuster, LLC
1230 Avenue of the Americas
New York, NY 10020

First Scribner trade paperback edition January 2026

Interior design by Kathryn A. Kenney-Peterson

Manufactured in the United States of America

1 3 5 7 9 10 8 6 4 2

Library of Congress Cataloging-in-Publication Data is available.

ISBN 978-1-6680-7840-2
ISBN 978-1-6680-7842-6 (ebook)

for all of Alice's children

"This is the politics of representation, where black subjectivity exists for its social and political meaningfulness rather than as a marker of the human individuality of the person who is black."

Kevin Quashie, *The Sovereignty of Quiet*

"I walk into the gallery like, bitch, I am the artshow."

Cure for Paranoia, "THE ARTSHOW"

TABLE OF CONTENTS

REVELATIONS

THE BOOK OF

ALICE

RECORD OF DEATHS: DIAMOND FORDE

or Written Apology to Me in a Parallel Universe

"Let's start the story backwards—" —Doechii

Like anyone with an imagination, I grieve
the infinite   me, a multiverse
of *self* thrust through space dust,

& I've survived

one drowning—lifted from the deep
by strange hands, sopping
air into my water-wrung lungs

        while a different Diamond
        in a different time
        kept sinking—

I am sorry

        that I have lived

through three car wrecks, two surgeries, & my own hand
capped on an oversized bottle of pain
meds,   which means I owe

another apology. To *you*, as in the other *me*,
forced to feed each pip down your longing.

I was too glad to tuck each sun like a clementine in my pocket.

        & I still don't know what it means to leave

a legacy of sputum,
or to nestle each night
in a catacomb, & lo!

for our multiverse sisters
who surely guarded Mama as she cried
in her closet, cornered by a cemetery of shoes—let Mercy

be a GOD who listens:

let me die
the way Grandma died: stroked out, stoked
on eucharistic commitments to

          me—   no, *you*—   a fantasy far
& hip-deep in daffodils, sunlight dribbling
down our chin:

the survivor
    left to pry these dream songs
            from the honeysuckle sky—

    promise you'll hold me

like a long, needful breath

    then turn me loose.

FAMILY TREE

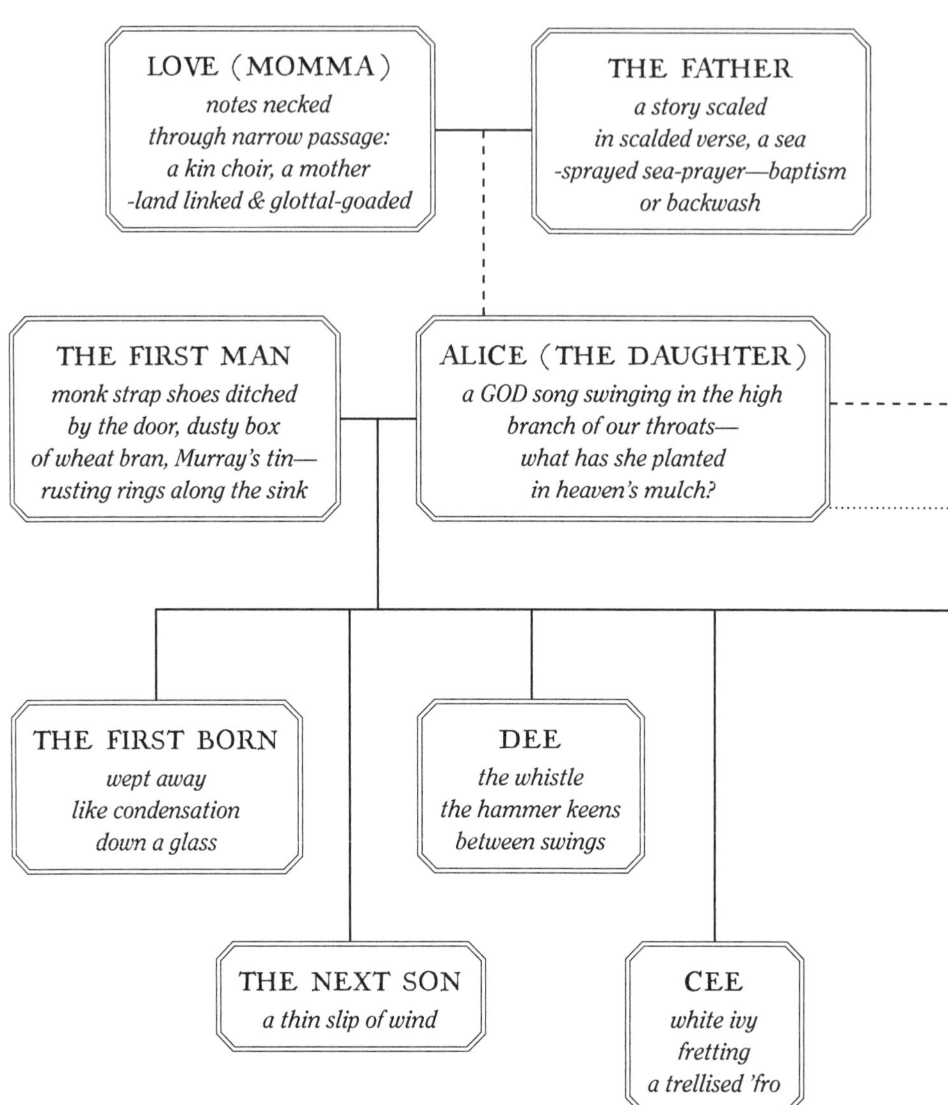

LOVE (MOMMA)
notes necked
through narrow passage:
a kin choir, a mother
-land linked & glottal-goaded
THE FATHER
a story scaled
in scalded verse, a sea
-sprayed sea-prayer—baptism
or backwash
THE FIRST MAN
monk strap shoes ditched
by the door, dusty box
of wheat bran, Murray's tin—
rusting rings along the sink
ALICE (THE DAUGHTER)
a GOD song swinging in the high
branch of our throats—
what has she planted
in heaven's mulch?
THE FIRST BORN
wept away
like condensation
down a glass
DEE
the whistle
the hammer keens
between swings
THE NEXT SON
a thin slip of wind
CEE
white ivy
fretting
a trellised 'fro

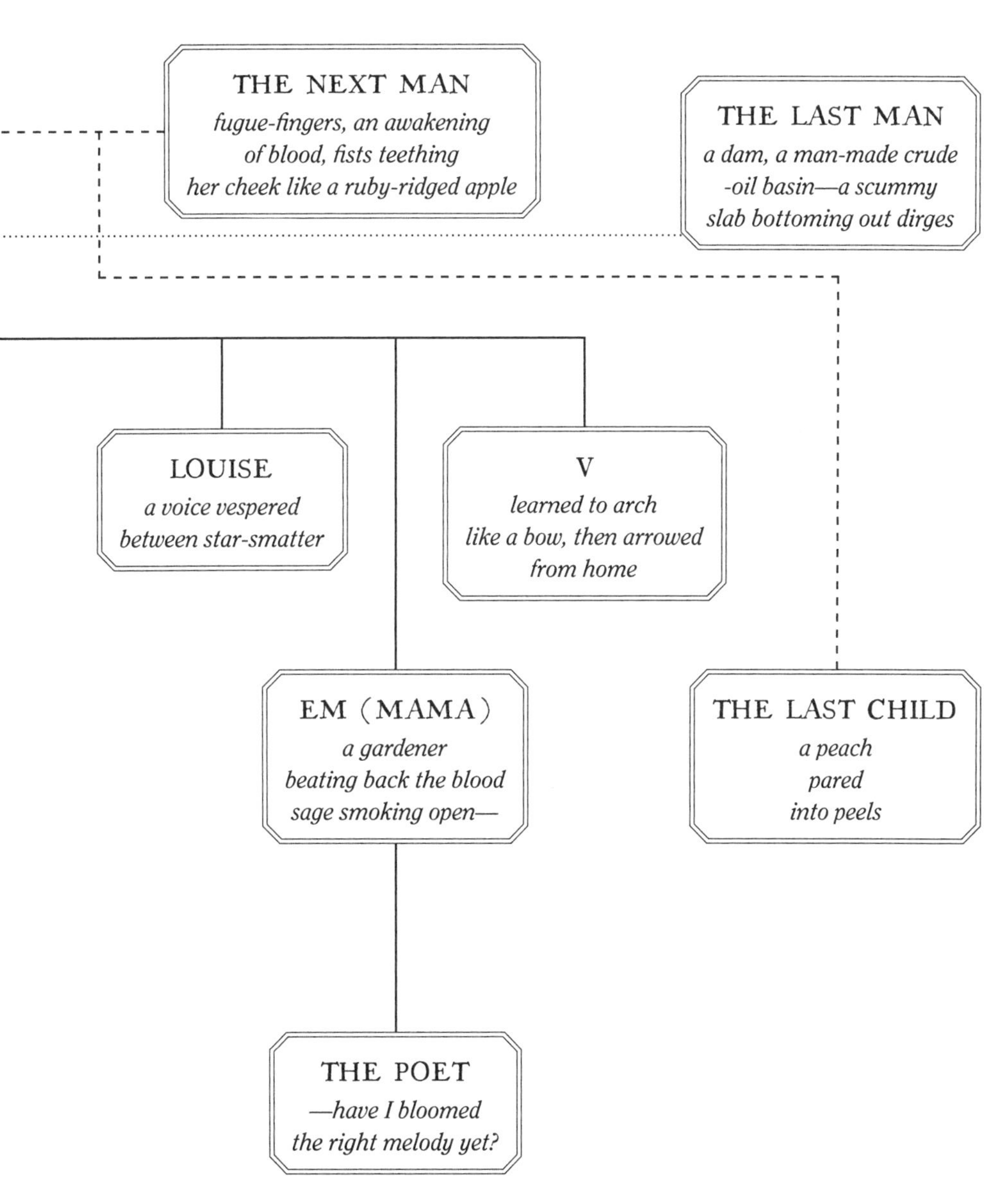
THE NEXT MAN
fugue-fingers, an awakening
of blood, fists teething
her cheek like a ruby-ridged apple
THE LAST MAN
a dam, a man-made crude
-oil basin—a scummy
slab bottoming out dirges
LOUISE
a voice vespered
between star-smatter
V
learned to arch
like a bow, then arrowed
from home
EM (MAMA)
a gardener
beating back the blood
sage smoking open—
THE LAST CHILD
a peach
pared
into peels
THE POET
—have I bloomed
the right melody yet?

GENESIS

CREATION MYTH: ALICE

IN the beginning, Alice dusted her counters with flour bleached enough to cloth the Carolinas.

2 Outside, sky treaded blue beneath the croon of a well-tuned garden, its hydrangea-hush blushed over breakfast's chorus: biscuits blaring their trumpet heads into the heat. Each morning, biscuits, then a cotton field proofing like dough.

3 Outside, Alice dodged the nipping stalks, her dress fanning like the unbroken wings of a sandhill crane—Alice dipped to unfix each boll with a twist, then unbent, her dark hair lagooning till, fed up, she wrapped the flooding coils into a basket around her arm.

4 In the beginning, Alice & her basket of curls culled the ghastly fields, dragged behind them the sun like a wet rag till the rows dampened with light.

5 At night, Alice simmered in the tub inside her yard. Tired in her tin bath's foundry, hooks still gutting her spine, Alice sank in white suds till the dark buds under her eyelids ghosted white, & the square tops of her toes pruned white, & her voice churned into white foam.

6 The first man to ask me to marry him, I will.

7 A mantra hymning a spell, charming the sugar in her cracked wheat, her boots' rubber heels, even the dirt sifting hillsides on the sill. The first man . . . the-first-man . . . the-first-man-I-will, she intoned, till her tongue wept magic, & The First Man sprouted, watered from the spittle of her wish.

8 In the beginning, Alice loved the man—his long stride a lyric, his jaw unhitched for song. He was the copper latch on a new set of luggage, a chrome grille mirroring the road,

9 & she would marry him, would carry his arias till they burst from her placental dreams with the force of a purpled, bleating GOD.

10 But The First Man wondered if she could sate his human hungers, so Alice reached for the bucket of lard in the icebox, its animal musk glistening up her wrists,

11 then laid the familiar landscape, the powder mountaining her countertop, buttermilk so cold her palm pads pinked like bougainvillea.

12 The secret to making biscuits
is that making biscuits is nothing
like loving a man.

13 The first time my grandparents held hands, Alice dawdled a finger past his rough patches, noticed a callus puckering where the joints met, same spot as hers, but ignored her urge to break open—

14 She had been taught to treat men like dough, to never overwork them, that a touch too much was a risk, could warp the golden bread into discs, like biting into a cotton-worn fist—

15 & this lesson must be true, Alice said, because what did she know about love except the silent corners a man left when he'd gone.

ORIGIN STORY: THE FATHER

THE Father bought a pair of oxfords—
cream-colored, copper heels beaming
like pennies—& kept them in a box in his car

& The Father would cart the box from his car
to The Street

& The Street watched. & the ladies on the porch
shucking pole beans from they stems watched.
& the wind, once dragged through the gray tops
of the houses, stuttered, then stopped

& The Father, hot, walked the watching
Street with a shoebox in his arms.

The Father knocked at The First House,
& at The First House was Grace.

But Grace didn't like shoes
in the house—the scuff & creak

on the hard floors. She lived quiet.
Spooned soup but never touched
the bowl. Mopped but wouldn't hum sweet
serenades to the suds—even with

a husband not home. Grace swore
silence was survival. Watched

mice scurry the crawl space as a girl.
Noticed, only, the squeaking ones

cogged in the moist machinery
of the tomcat's mouth.

When Grace saw The Father at her door,
necktie noosed around the milky giblets
of his neck, she refused to open,
not even for the sun to tiptoe in.

& The Father, hot, walked the watching
Street with a shoebox in his arms.

The Father knocked at The Next House,
& at The Next House was Joy.

Joy walked in midnight
& the moon followed. Joy whistled

from the breath of many men. Hips wide
as lampshades—Joy held her own light,
shined in the frame while her kids lapped
the living room behind, laughter rattling the rails.

& The Father said, Good evenin'.
& Joy regarded him with the confidence of women

taught to be fruit
on a high branch, & The Father blanched,

fumbled with the box topped in his arms,
asked, Can I sale you some shoes?

& Joy said, Nahsir, & her voice jangled
like a pocketbook full of Susan Bs,
capital in her honey jar, saved herself
bread for her own garden to tend—

& The Father, hot, walked the watching
Street with a shoebox in his arms.

The Father knocked at The Last House,
& at The Last House was Love.

Love, too, was beautiful, even when summer scuttled
over her like a winched field of rye.

Love ushered The Father inside, poured him coffee
& a clap of cream in the tapered mug he liked.
Love didn't mind. The Father didn't sell shoes—not really.
This was 1930—before The Father was allowed

to hold Love like a thrasher in his snowbanked
palms. But how he longed to hold her—GOD

rustled in her skirts & he had to know
what heaven looked like, had to kiss

the open vase of her brown lips, the gospel budding
between them, & when she spoke his name

The Father felt divine, like the power he held
was his the whole time—
& together Father & Love brought forth creatures
in their likeness, called one Daughter,

took the oxfords
from the box & left them for her

while GOD plucked
a hangnail from his thumb.

& The Daughter, in her hard shoes, watched
her Father leave with a shoebox in his arms.

CLABBER MILK CORNBREAD

or How to Keep The Daughter Humble

INGREDIENTS

2 cups cornmeal	an egg (wrestled warm from the hen)
full pan bacon fat	3/4ths cup of butter, soft
2 cups clabber milk, cold	a sugared pinch
1 teaspoon baking soda & salt	a cast-iron, screaming hot

DIRECTIONS

1. Soak the cornmeal in the clabber jar overnight to loosen its toothsome bite—but only if it's stone-ground. (& it will be. Hurled upon the WORD each day, she'll learn ta dodge the pebbled sky.)

2. & when she's five, show her the pigpen, the Yorkshire glazed bored in the mud. She'll hope ta play, ta ride him in The Blue to the pond you love—the old hole your Daddy dug back when you, too, was proud—ashy—unabashedly loud, dodging the rough hands you called brothers

back before the catfish learned ta bend like reeds, tryna hide from your greasy gathering—half ya Daddy's family bunched under a fish fry's rank.

Her fingers rake against the hem on her hip, a twitch, a wish to itch the swine behind his flitting ears. Swat her. Not hard, just enough ta startle her from wanting. Then show her Mercy—cut the neck so clean, the blood forgets to leap into its red skirt. She'll tremble, awestruck, in her feathers. Tell her this is the first of many blessings.

3. Fry the bacon till it kicks, sputtering, the pig's last will & testament. These leachings, the foundation on which you'll build.

4. Crack the egg. Mix with steady hand. (& you'll be steady. So steady, she'll mistake you for a god. Your Father, just as unflappable. Couldn't move from drink till drink moved him from you. & Pastor say he watchin', but you hope GOD's good enough ta shut the curtain the day you conceived

5. a dream—your Daughter, taffeta-curled & thrown into cast-iron summer. She runs & you fix ta catch her but she sizzles between your fingers like drippings, dress flapping, footsteps fervid & far-flung—she's an auric pleat of laughter, a seamed bright sun, & you) bake (in a kind of devotion, remember the flickering embers of your Daddy's eyes turned coal—if you could smote the light blinking on her back, if you could bear the burn, an old flame winking in her smile—maybe, just maybe, you could keep her.)

BILDUNGSROMAN WITH A LINE BY FRANCES E. W. HARPER

IN the BOOK of ESTHER,
before the banquets & gallows, disses & decrees,
there lived a Persian king & his queen-wife, Vashti.

& it came to pass that the Persian king, drunk
on every muscadine wine his feasting could find,
sent his seven chamberlains to fetch the queen-wife,

Vashti that she might stand full-beauty in front of them
(naked, some say)—because she moved with the ease
of a skiff boat scissoring waves into lace, & the king kept

Vashti as an amphora vase: bangled wrists fixed to her dark hips,
an inch from breaking. But who could seek to hold a woman
who cooled through their palms like rain?

When Vashti shunned the summons, stunning
the chamberlains seven, her birthright lit like a pyre.
Thus, the wroth king wrecked his banquet like a jilted gale

& the chamberlains warned him that the women
would hear of this—would shuck, slight, or outright scorn
their husbands—& that the king would need to strip

Vashti of her crown (none know how—banishment?
easing her perfect neck beneath the blade?).
There would be no one left to warn us after Vashti.

*

So when The Daughter finished the BOOK,
tucked its binding beside her breast, then pressed
fast to the barn out back, ducked dogwood—

old bark peeling in the breeze—found Momma
shoveling straw into the goat's stalls, then thinned
the Bible between them, asked Momma why

Vashti hadn't heeded the kingly summons,
what could Momma tell The Daughter
about the pain of awakening

to yourself? It would come to pass, in time.
The Daughter, chucking girlhood like a ticket stub,
becoming Alice—another woman

lick-spittled by sorrow, forge-spit into someone
who could bend to grief, but would not bow for shame.
Maybe The Daughter could've decided different,

become, instead, an inhibition
of clover—a spring shoot
leafing out wood ash—a dandelion

splitting the sidewalk's teeth. Someone unkempt
as the threats that will make her, a wilderness
sprigging vicious in her chest.

LOT'S WIFE

THE truth is, I'd do it again—turn into the winking eye
of a city flushed with fire. I hope I burn this time,
my body curling like the ruffled apron
on the hook, the pen-scratched books, the candles
cindered to scents. At least let me be
turmeric—cardamom—saffron sprinkling from heaven
like the dandruff of Mars. I want to be a spice
men burn for. I want to be architecture, the pillar
of a temple where men line to floss their tongues
on the salt snowing my truss. Salt cathedral. Salt
palace. Mountaintops crusted with salt. Country
whose borders are diamonds of salt or the salted coast
of a continent, its oceans full of the bones of women
like me, whose tombs are the only homes we keep—
GOD, give me a name worth remembering.

POEM IN WHICH I SHOULD WRITE ABOUT CAIN, BUT I'M TIRED OF WRITING ABOUT DEATH

SO instead, a houseplant arching a trellis
of its own strong stems, elephant ear,
Colocasia, what my Aunt Cee called *Alice*,
ready for the sure mothering
of her own mother. She tended Alice
with the surgical heed of a woman
seaming silver to the sharp ends
of the moon, & even when she yelled at us
for crawling through the jungle-mess
of Alice's large leaves, when we scattered soil
so far she'd find perlite wedged inside
the treadmill, sometimes she'd still let me
water or cull the gilded curls
of a dead sprout hung like a wrung-out
washcloth, & in my hands, I think she saw
a potential to dig, to muck deep
into the manure of my imagination, to sprout
offshoots I'll plant in someone else
someday, when I am not afraid
to think of myself as a god large enough
that every heart-shaped leaf dicing light
to dust could beat in my own chest,
& I've never made a life, but I've reached
into the refuse they make of us,
found hearts hardy as crocus bulbs,
& in this poem I will plant a world for women
where kudzu climbs & is wanted.

COURTIN'

WE giggle by the wet banks,
laughter flirting with the shadowed
wood—he's smooth, scoops his hand
like a shovel against my back,

catches my glances, & I discover it
etched in the black uncharted
mapped behind his eyes & that's why
I let him do it—take me

like a mother, meaning
he reminds me of my smallness
of a chickadee, twig-fragile, & in his hands
I imagine starlight, berbere & yeast,

a whole world whistling between his arms,
& when he leans in, I gasp, bend,
crown into his collarbone, chew
at the cigar stank bejeweling his nape,

& maybe us songbirds
sangin' an agrestic gospel,
or maybe us a melody of sky—
cuz when he kiss me, it's communion:

the sum of us pecked into sugar,
& when he say he wants me
to be his woman, he means we two players
in a game already rule-bound & gender-mercied,

that I will give as much as he takes,
the same impossible game
my Momma's Mommas played, & maybe
that's why when us two part, I already know

who's won.

EXODUS

ON THE TRAIN TO NEW YORK

This is how Alice will come to understand leaving:
the stains of Carolina beaten from her shoes
till only the haunting remained—

ALICE presses her back into the red brick
of the railway station. Beneath her, the earth
whets its hips into the wheels of the coming
train, & the train squeals back with hunger.

When the train stops, Alice stares
into the window's glittering teeth, tries to
cast the light within as something warm
like a pillow still damp with dreaming.

The First Man hangs his hands on her neck,
then together they cart into the train's mouth,
baggage clacking loud like a lock clamped shut.

The hills are the first to understand
that Alice is leaving. It's all they know—
have known the Daughters, too,

housed in their vales, heard their laughter
as it aged into the netted veil of memory
too soon—so when Alice steps on the train

the hills billow their backs, they shove
their green hips against the tracks, they shake
till the teacups rattle & the wealthy wilt like daisies in their skirts.

But fear not, it is GOD who eases the earth.
Thus saith the LORD GOD unto the Mount, Let my people go
that they might altar these valleys, that their children might heal

the scars ridged deep in these hills,
& the hillsides, sated by the sweet meat of His WORD,
curled into their grassy spines to sleep.

The cicadas are the second to understand
that Alice is leaving. They do what they know
how to do: mourn—the same sorrowful song

for generations. When the first tree crashed
on the rain-splashed mattress of the forest floor,
some say it was the cicadas, moaning from the mud,

that reverbed the earth into a mishmash after,
trebled land from mass to a slapdash of continents
so that when Alice crams her suitcase between her feet

the cicadas' screech syncs with the train's beat
& a great yowl straddles the trees, rips, even, the linen
sky, then porter & passenger plug their ears & cry.

But fear not, GOD hears the lamentation.
Thus saith the LORD of crackle & creek, Let my people go
that they may mourn their mom & pop idols:

shelves of sunny peaches, boiled peanuts, sweet potatoes
golden as a harp. & the cicadas, soothed in the river spilt
from GOD's jaw, bend their heads to drink.

The train wheels its final warning. The flora jostle,
stretch their green necks to see Alice, who they know
must be weeping to lose them—what a surprise

to find her eyes still dry—& like wildfire, a rage blazes
& the fields burst into golden glory, sneezeweed, yellow
rockets bright enough to stun the conductor

who jolts, sure that he's crashing into the sun,
& when the train lurches, fear bullets the fauna:
the dogs yowl, the chickens clack, the titmouse peter-peters

through his woe-doused stretch of wood—
& when the talons trap him, he hears the horned owl's nocturne
turn aubade for the first time.

But fear not, for GOD divided light from dark.
Thus saith the LORD GOD of the gladsome garden, Let my people go
that they might bloom fields from the doll's-eyes

of their brood. & the flowers, scolded,
simmer into a less dazzling mood.

Only the fish seem truly happy—
shad & crappie, walleye & carp,
so unbothered by Alice's leaving,

the fish throw themselves a fete,
a ruckus, a brouhaha bubbling up beneath
The Blue—even the trout undress

from their beer-batter, but
the LORD GOD demands decorum,
so gathered the puddles, the ponds,

the rivers, & the seas. Thus saith the aqua GOD,
Remember, my people will go
to feast upon the bounty of their futures,

then the croaker & bass, perch,
pike, & catfish dip behind their fins
& grin.

Humidity understands nothing about leaving.
She will never let go, hangs by the wayside
when Alice walks past, coaxes a boar-

bristle brush through her 'fro. There is nowhere
her curls can't coil, they kiss even the backside
of Alice's throat, so that when Alice kicks back

into the COLORED section, Humidity settles in, too,
tucks a coil behind her ear, then pours everywhere,
over the babies in their baskets, & the white men
glossy beneath their herringbone hats.

But fear not, GOD is a cool hand. He sends
the zephyr down. Thus saith the LORD GOD of the breeze,
Please let my people go

that they may baptize in the murky fount of a fire
hydrant, that their cherubs might worship summer
with their toes splashing in the stream.

But Humidity don't listen. She holds even Him
in her grotesque heat. She opens the window,
pours patiently into the liquid dark.

Alice watches what was once hills sharpen
into houses, the stars shimmer with exhaust,
the horizon she once knew:

foaming waves of white—now buried
under skyscrapers, factory smoke, a cityscape
sketched through a cotton-dirtied sky.

Alice removes her shoes from her sore feet,
flexes her tired toes, then cups the right boot
in her left palm, peers for inspection,

sees in the well-worn tread a bit of Carolina clay
nipped between the grooves. She plucks the mud up,
pinches its rosy trails between her fingers

—that last remnant of home.

SOUTHERN FRIED CATFISH

or How to Disguise a Carolinian in New York

INGREDIENTS

8 skinned catfish, cut
1 quart oil
buttermilk thickened with egg
cornmeal & flour, sifted & seasoned
an iron skillet
a hankering for home

DIRECTIONS

1. Stroll up to your monger as he somersaults the brine-stink of the sea
into an ice chest. Ask him for two pounds of catfish, & if his nose puckers
like a pickled plum, he'll call it *mud cat, polliwog, bottom-feeder*
of the bog—just pretend he ain't talking about you.

2. Soak fillets in buttermilk
till the fish forgets
it never was a fish,
that it never knew a scale
could cast diamonds
into so much broken light—

3. Combine cornmeal in a small dish with all your spices. Remember Momma's hand
heavy on the seasonin' salt—how you used to want to lick her thumb clean
of the Bay, tongue stiff & prodding your teeth like a crawfish castle.

4. Heat the oil but say it slow, don't let the *o* gloss inside your throat—*oil*—the
tongue twister of boil, of pin & pen—say it like you belong. Say it again. Then again.

5. When you first moved to the Big City, you bought a bolt of black cloth,
stitched a dress with gold & silver ends, & everywhere you went
you smelled money. Naïve enough to still be rich
with possibility, you paced from bodega to bus stop,
clip-clopped in those cheap & squeaky heels
till the blisters popped & the whole block heard
your dogs bark—

Bread the catfish. Shake the excess.

6. Fry the fish in batches. Sing a little Stella till the grease hiss. Tell the LORD *you*
don't have ta move my mountain—you will move from them yourself.

CALLIN' THE HOGS

HE ain't coming back tonight. Next night neither. You hear your marrow
cresting its cricks & miss what you never thought you'd miss: him
snoring through midnight, uvula clocking its knocker on his throat's narrow
door. The hogs housed in his hothouse mouth—whose truffle they rootin'

now? You collage women in your sleep: knees nylon-sleeved, wrists angled
to hips, ears clamped 'round his late-night sounds—those women a fly-
trap & he the fly. You head outside in a bathrobe blue & moth-mangled,
find a patch of grass green enough to dream itself a field, then lie

down, nipple the fang-toothed moon, unseed the pale buttons fastening
your ribs till the bones axe dark. Your chest basins to a trough,
unctuous butter of your esophagus flushed & fattening,
your lungs sear like a fillet in the heat. Buffet of pinks, your heart dins

its dinner-bell but you don't care if he potbellies home to eat.
You just want a whiff ta wander in'm. He should know he's missed a feast.

THE FIRST BORN

& the LORD said unto the womb of Alice, Sing! & the uterus bellowed its trumpet, & the tubes rattled their maracas, & the eggs clattered their ovarian gourds.

2 Sometimes The First Man would hymn his lips on Alice, would croon a tune she couldn't sing alone, & it was then she saw him the way other women saw him, like a finger fluttering her valves.

3 Sometimes The First Man would wander, so Alice went to bed with the sheets heaped into the shape of him, tried to ignore the bedside candle oscillating its anemone-scented eye.

4 Alice longed to tip that candle. To let its fire silk its glossy slip around her. Heat, Alice thought, is the birthplace of living, but she could hardly remember the summered hills that raised her, could hardly remember anything that wasn't the smell of him: Newports & nickels, someone's perfume petaling like a kiss along his chin.

5 Another night The First Man wandered, & it was then that Alice could hear the trains screech their metal nocturnes outside her window, the dogs wheel their whirling howl, a stranger's voice spindling through the wood floors.

6 Then Alice said unto the LORD, Lo! that I should love a man in parts—that I should want him even for his fingers when I cannot have his heart.

7 & the LORD said unto Alice, Just make what you want, so Alice jammed her hand into the pitch between her legs, pulled the song GOD nested there—melody of a dark child black with blood, throat wet & red as a melon—

8 & Alice pressed the song-child to her chest, fed him honeyed milk from her breast, & the child's cheeks sucked & billowed like linen on the line. Alice stained warm by his lapping tongue.

9 & in the dewy eye of the streetlights, Alice & her song-child slept to the *snik-snik* of a hunger quenched.

WHAT TO DO WITH YOUR HANDS WHILE DANCING

THE First Born laid his hands upon his sister's shoulders,
showed her how to shake the predatory gaze of the moon,

cuz he knew enough about himself to lead his sister Em
to the rhythm of her own discovery, the two of them

dipping like drinking elk, her crown & cackle rising up
to brush against heaven's bottom. Black folk know GOD

in the first notes of a good tune, footwork—a kind of labor.
Sometimes to dance is to mourn with your whole body.

The day The First Born died—Em's eyes tangoed
through the dance halls, stepping on the heels of her shadow.

Why not hold to the kick of another's heart while you can hear it?
Why not lose yourself in the unshackled lineage of song?

The First Born hurricaned his hips over the hull of evening,
gliding like a tugboat on a river of smoke.

U.S. DEPARTMENT OF COMMERCE
BUREAU OF THE CENSUS:
1960 CENSUS OF POPULATION AND HOUSING

or Census Sonnet

NAME	RELATIONSHIP	RACE
~~The First Man~~	~~*HEAD*~~	In my bedroom, we guard a nest for wasps between the window & screen, obscene
Alice	*Wife*	red wasps whipping a papery aria for weeks till my man returned
The First Born	*Son*	well-armed with a can of Raid, placed between glass & bated breath
Dee	*Daughter*	waitin' ta spring, he shouts at me ta count the wasps, so I do
The Next Son	*Son*	count each quick-tick reflex leaving their wings—fifteen wasps made cemetery
Cee	*Daughter*	on the sill, bodies curling like rose petals— but I am counting still—
Louise	*Daughter*	a strangeness swarmy in my chest— for the first time, I can number my dead.

DAUGHTERS

CENSUS OF DAUGHTERS

& these are the Daughters of The First Man: Daughters who dream of organza veils & wake to pray. Daughters of breast milk. Daughters of strata. Daughters of kaolin clay. Daughters under throw & wheel, Daughters whose birth mugs a mother's will—

Thus Dee—daughter of wombwork, daughter of war. Daughter who plaits deft & dagwood, hands weave blisters down her sisters' scalps. A mother-wish for sweetness, Dee decks her bullies, then blackens the rum cake with Alaga syrup.

Then Cee—next daughter. Daughter of hymn, of hallelujah, of hand-me-downs, daughter whose bowed head didn't lift for decades. Cee blinks & guitar strings plink coins in her ear well, their clatter cantoring a timeworn cantata for riches.

Thus Louise, daughter of harpsichord, daughter of aria. Broadway & gospel warrior. Daughter who brandished her blade-belly tongue, who cut the umbilical wart, gaped the gap in its bruise-black mouth—swore she saw her own mother peek out.

Then Em, star-tinseled daughter. Daughter whose eyelashes fan like a tarot deck. Daughter of spirit realm, of night watch, of sleepless tick: Em scopes ghosts strung up like cobwebs in the corner cuz Em be the GOD bride. Em wear the veil. Em sees

what V must feel—cuz V be body. V be young. V be a tooth warmed in a dusk-gored plum—a snack, bikini-brilliant, posted up in the sand—but V don't touch the water. Swimming is not dreaming, is not flight, & V is bird bones—she jumps & floats—be

an in-between—exactly what her mother wished for but ain't—every daughter the same: stardust—even Alice—a daughter: shimmering in circles, feeding on maternal heat—exactly what a Daughter be: a black hole gulping up love.

COLLARD GREENS & HAM HOCKS

or What to Do When the Bills Are Due

INGREDIENTS

3 bunches collards	1 chopped onion
one dab bacon fat	Lawry's, pepper, salt
smoked hocks	apple cider vinegar
chicken stock	the really deep pot

DIRECTIONS

1. ablute the bunches, free the greens
from their bitter spines, then twine

them 'round your fingers, fret
the rugged ends—your Daughters'

edges leafing from their box braids already,
the dark hairs wildin' like vines.

you twist
their tresses,

plant your tired thumbs
against their roots

they always bloom too soon

2. tease the skin back, watch
the onion flirt open, hungry

for touch. affix the knife. dice,
a sting singing loudly in your cuts—like a Daughter

when she asks why you're never around
on holidays, at family dinners,

at school plays, birthdays, her adolescence
an album of snapshots without you

3. & it isn't because you don't miss them
though you have wanted less

have even enjoyed
the salt broth your distance makes but

they are always with you
& you hook each minimum-wage minute on

the sharp end of their frowns—

4. start a pot as deep as your empty pocket
sauté the onions, a clot of grease leaping

in the heat. toss the ham hocks in
the chicken stock, the salt

pork pearled into fat, vinegar,
& spice—twice

y'all dined in candlelight, your Daughters
haloed & sweat-strung, you

braising all day,
but tonight y'all will eat in heaps—greens

spilling wild as an animal—greens
like a grief come home, just spilling

past pot & powder milk pantry, past
sparkless socket—an eagerness of greens

smearing down every wall you've built.

SETHE SPEAKS TO HAGAR

WE was girls, once. Our mornings, pebbles &
goose feathers, sweat glitterin' like bracelets
on our wrists, only a monster could look

us in our dream-doped eyes to tell us
one day, our mornings would be animal work,
the kind that scoops ya spine like a mule,

& our nights would fang us jammy bruises
on our necks. How many stars did ya count
through the net of your Mr's hands before ya stopped

believin' in the places he couldn't reach?
After you ran & the rivers rose ta stop you, the deserts
spanned ta stop you, the mountains pointed at your neck—

of course, ya came back—even when GOD promised
us a nation of bone. We's women, now.
Every time we bleed, it's for somebody we love.

WOMANING

LOVE, GOD say, is obedience, so I obey
the alarm of sun sung through my window,
climb down cold steps ta hymn & hem, ta cook,
clatter, & kid myself into believing these tasks
don't hook familiar shackles, & when my man
kiss me in the soft spot below my ear, I dream
he really want me, but that's what's wrong
with womanin', we stay spinning yarn
from the colorful crochet of our minds, but few
admire it—Dear LORD, why did you make me
in your image if you wanted me ta kneel?
Let me break the rules one time, lace the loafers
by the front door on my large, girlish feet,
then walk like I got somewhere, everywhere, to go.

FAT GOSPEL

THE first time Alice realized that she was fat, she was nursing—her Last Child latched & holing in her folds—& it was then that Alice noticed how well her nursed child molded to her mother, cuddled too comfortably in her arms.

But maybe this is motherhood, too, Alice decided. Maybe she had adapted to lift a child's heft, & so now the two of them could hum brilliant in the milk hush, her infant well-fed & rested.

& it came to pass that Alice was fine with her fat.

*

The second time Alice realized that she was fat, she was prepping supper—butter beans & turkey wings—& so packed into the pantry for a can of limas when The Next Man

stepped behind & scooped her into him, a purr burbling on low boil in his throat, massaged the flesh banded against her wrists, his famished hands moving down to her hips, & when she snorted, her hips bounced between them like rubber. Alice startled, new to how a body could whimsy wide at another man's wish.

But maybe this is a woman wonder, too, Alice decided. Maybe fat is who she was meant to be, each expanse—a body reactive, acclimation to the adamant demands of love—yes, The Next Man needed softness, & so did she.

& it came to pass that Alice was fine with her fat.

*

The third time Alice realized that she was fat, she was at the evening service, plunked down creaking in a pew beside the deacon's wife—who the church girls called *Ma'am*, instinctively reverent to the judgment made obvious in her smile.

Ma'am rose to greet Alice & Alice stood, waiting to be pulled in, to feel Ma'am's permed & pin-bobbed head digging in her shoulder, then felt a shudder, so jerked back, noticed her skin had swelled to pucker itself around Ma'am's ear, like it meant to suck the cartilage clear from her head—

then Alice jumped, & Ma'am feathered in her silk hat, & the fat, a half inch thick now, quickened to comfort.

When Alice looked at Ma'am, she knew that Ma'am had seen enough. She smiled that reverent smile, then moved back to her pew, & Alice leaned back in her booth, trying to will the red meat back to the bone.

*

& it had come to pass that the fat would have to go.

Though it would know no leaving. Despite diets & walks & midnight talks in the bathroom mirror trying to smack her belly back. Despite the gazes scissoring through her in the neighborhood, their eyes carving to the quick—the fat stayed true.

From summer to winter, from avenue to street, through the whole damn breach of New York, Alice widened but never to her liking, flounced at the world's whim but never for her own. What would it feel like, Alice wondered, ta belong ta myself again?

*

The last time Alice cared that she was fat, she was running errands, walked the print-littered sidewalks coming up past studios, suit shops, neared a Black girl young enough to be her middle child, & the child, fixed on a decades-old mink sitting pretty in the boutique, mashed her nose against the glass, flowering up roses of mist.

The girl longed for the coat, the way Alice once longed
for lavish evenings, for diamond earrings, for long gloves
the color of a midnight merlot—to burn under any star-

dream far from the shared room in her childhood home,
secretly tucking away newspaper scraps of faraway
lands in her nightstand, already aware that some dreams

she couldn't afford, & that some hungers
could never be sated. When Alice, then the Daughter, reached
for a second piece of chicken & her sister's smile slid

across her plate, asked *You sure 'bout that?*
what could the Daughter do except swallow
her wanting, keep it in the damp dream dark of her throat?

*

& when Alice looks at the girl again, smiling beneath her tattered toboggan, Alice remembers for the first time

her urge for wings

& it was as if her body were always waiting.

For muscle memory, or an old whim punched through her winter coat, the fat unfettered & feathering, tendons fingering out from the
shoulder blades, wefted into brown-banded wings—

Alice flew.

*

Feet untethered to any north she knew, Alice kept floating, yelping through that impossibility of blue, & when she reached back, saw the small girl watching, her chin affixed in silent song, the girl reached, too, hands twittering like a bird in flight &—

*

what then
do you want to happen?

the landing? the liftoff,
just a twin streak fleeing

for sky? What ending
is safe enough

for them to be in?
Better to protect

this moment
in perpetuity—the two of them

unlimited   as the bauble of stars
hitched always to their heels

ANOTHER DAMN BODY POEM

THE second Alice's Studebaker stuttered from the lot to the night service, where the gospel choir paddled through their tidal couplets of piety & prayer, the Daughters stay behind to watch each other nose a needle over the forbidden record their cousins smuggled in under their shirts.

2 Rhythm & blues, the tunes Alice banned with The First Man—if she could see them now: in her house tinseling the stairway in Earth, Wind & Fire, canopies filigreed in Isley Brothers, The Spinners spinning through the rooms—

3 while the cousins circled the floor-length mirror in the girls' room, shirts tied, checkered & paisley button-ups bonneting their midriffs

4 then the Daughters, too, the whole girl-gaggle flicking their otter bodies to the guitar's pulse, wanting thick hips & a boy with hands capped like a minaret against them

5 all this exploration, till The Next Son's voice creaked from the stairwell—well-placed lookout for the pecan-colored putter of Alice's jalopy plunking up the drive. Then the music stopped. & the evening quieted back in.

6 Once, while the Daughters danced together in their bedroom, V, an infant then, crawled away from the groove to taste each splintered offering of her home world: the mango-sweetness of a dining set, cambric Brillo of an ottoman pressed against the gums, then beneath the sink, V gulping down the roach spray, an alarming whiteness bubbling up at the corners of her mouth.

7 When they found V, the Daughters panicked—already afraid of what they could say to Alice to explain how she had missed the preamble to her daughter's death. What could they do except stop the music, untie their checkered shirts, feed the baby a glass of milk, then fall to their knees to pray?

8 & fortunately, the youngest didn't die that day. By sunrise, V was well enough to nub the blue end of a plastic schooner toy between her budding teeth—

9 but the Daughters were done with mirrors.

10 Though I have sometimes wished I could take them back to the gyre & jive, to discovering they are the sunrise blotting Monet's blue wharf—my mother, Em, among them—too young to dance but old enough to already believe love was something never meant for her.

11 Our bodies, our temples—shouldn't that mean anyone can worship, shouldn't that mean that it's okay to dip my hips, spill, like a Communion bowl.

12 I confess, I was nearly twenty before I could touch myself the first time, my hands trembling like a weaverbird against the tightly woven nest.

13 Didn't I deserve to understand my below as more than blood home? as more than the hard weeks I spent on my bedroom floor hooded around a portable heater, praying the heat could ooze through, burn brighter than the white-hot pain of a uterus cauliflowered by tumors—

14 & the first time that I tried to die was because of this—because I couldn't sum my body beyond its nettle, its needled pins—

15 What I wouldn't have given then for a toe hair ode, or uterine elegy, a ballad of lopsided breasts—any mortal warble louder than the ache I knew inside me.

16 What does it mean that even now, I hate my body—hate that I'm still afraid of what I don't know about it, & that I write because I am afraid I might be that girl again—sprawled out on the bedroom floor, loathing the muscle-clench, the pang of body for some supposed man's due.

17 What I wouldn't have given then to shed my skin, to emerge new & pink-gleaming, reach for the translucent shell of my old self, gatored elbow & pebbled knee—dimpled chin & fat gut—hapless—how to make her happy except by plastering her on every page I think is mine—doesn't every body deserve to feel wanted?

ARS POETICA WITH SNOW GLOBES

after Martin & Muñoz's Sleepwalker, 2019

THE evergreens, sliced like perfect limes, lean
against the hill's snowy crescendo. A dog

fumbles down the powdered slopes, drags his paws
through polyurethane snow, tries to trail

the sleepwalker, his owner, her bare feet slapping
against a frostbitten hem, her arms outstretched

as if reaching for the wiry bridge of Grandma's
hands—in the hospital room, the coldness

of her grip in mine, I squeeze
into a hospital chair greased with mourning, pretend

I don't know the truth:
that when Grandma died, I prayed

at the altar of *Will & Grace* on a couch in my basement
miles away. That while the rest of my family

dragged their sorrow through the last wet breath
she left us, I was watching Jack eat lunch

with a Barbie doll made to look like Cher,
who he loved, but not enough to know her

when she was right in front of him, the real
Cher, fur-lined, bodied, but I understood Jack then

because this is how I learned to love, too,
doggedly chasing my fakes:

Grandma posed like a perfect doll
in my brain's pink playhouse.

How many times have I nuzzled my weathered mind
for forgiveness, nosed her out with a single scent,

how I dipped down in the fading hint of heat,
her imprint. I'm still chasing shadows.

LAMENTATIONS

PINEAPPLE-COCONUT CAKE

WHY didn't I celebrate you that night : when my cousins leaned across your nursing home bed to paint your mouth bright pink : who'd know this'd be the last time I could count each opal tooth : pineapple bright as a beachside : tinned for home, aluminum hum still clung to the fruit : on birthdays, you ate the biggest slice of cake : your indefinite origins : doctors unsure if you'd been born July first or fourth : four days you'd eat cake, then wait for the country to circle their bonfires, their billowing grills—fireworks shrilling brilliant off the house tops on the hill : feels like they celebrating me / with me, you said : & though you never read poetry, maybe a Clifton song mambas through all of us : so strong, I might forget the shape of the hurt I nursed : seeing you for the first time in years : guilt goosed in our necks : none of us loving you enough : to home you : but you had new places to be anyway : your spirit freighted through the phone wires while I, standing in front of you, went hungry for the sweet treat of your smile : mashed into doughy cheeks : a half grimace : as if you reigned : even the corners of your mouth : let that hunger carry me anywhere : the hood of my parents' hatchback, where the two of us leaned back & scooped with plastic spoons the coconut flaking our lips : celebratory stars smoking their multicolored spokes in the night : LOOK DOWN : but the voice is a wish inside me : I dare not : your mouth, smudged into sloppy lipstick—pink as the throat of GOD—bursts through

PORTRAIT OF MY GRANDMOTHER AS LAKE LURE IN WINTER

I wanted to lie for you   to whitewash the ashen meadow
of your crown   your light-dappled brow
even the clouds behind your eyes   bleached winter

is a soft-stepped past dampened with snow
but I've been yearning for the moment before
the break   before the switch became a switchblade   before memory

became a twig once daggered with ice   knifed roots piercing
& you never told Mama you loved her
          so even the trees have teeth the mountain fanged

with birch bone-white & yawning
& maybe you didn't love me neither
          maybe family was nothing to you

but sheet ice holding your head underwater
but I wish I didn't believe in the you that I've been painting
pinkmouthed gasping out   love   there is only quiet here

a lure with no line to pull   no blue-gilled thrashing
no birdsong no deer bramble duck babble no mosquito hiss
just me   pretending it is you mumbling in the morning

breeze   you left me   nothing
to find in these hills no chipmunk chatter on chinquapin
trees no beetle bustle   salamander slither   no jessamine

jumping up fence posts   just me
          & an outstretched hand
                    bitten by cold

THE RIGHT WORDS

ON the living room floor,
cutting your face from the family
photos, I handle the slices
of your severed head with the same
care GOD saves to end her children.

With the right words I, too,
can leave the devil in tears.
The lesson you taught me,
though I have forgotten
what it is I'm supposed to say.

I ask my sister
if she recalls the night
you prayed over me.
No, she says, *but we must have*
really had some demons in us.

I've been taught I can speak
anything into existence,
if I admit the evil I'm harboring,
I will become it. I will dip

the delicate flames of my lashes,
ignite the magnesium moon—
I don't fear destruction
but my love for it.

I want nothing more than the ease
to carve you out of me.

WHAT ALICE SAW

after Kenzie Allen

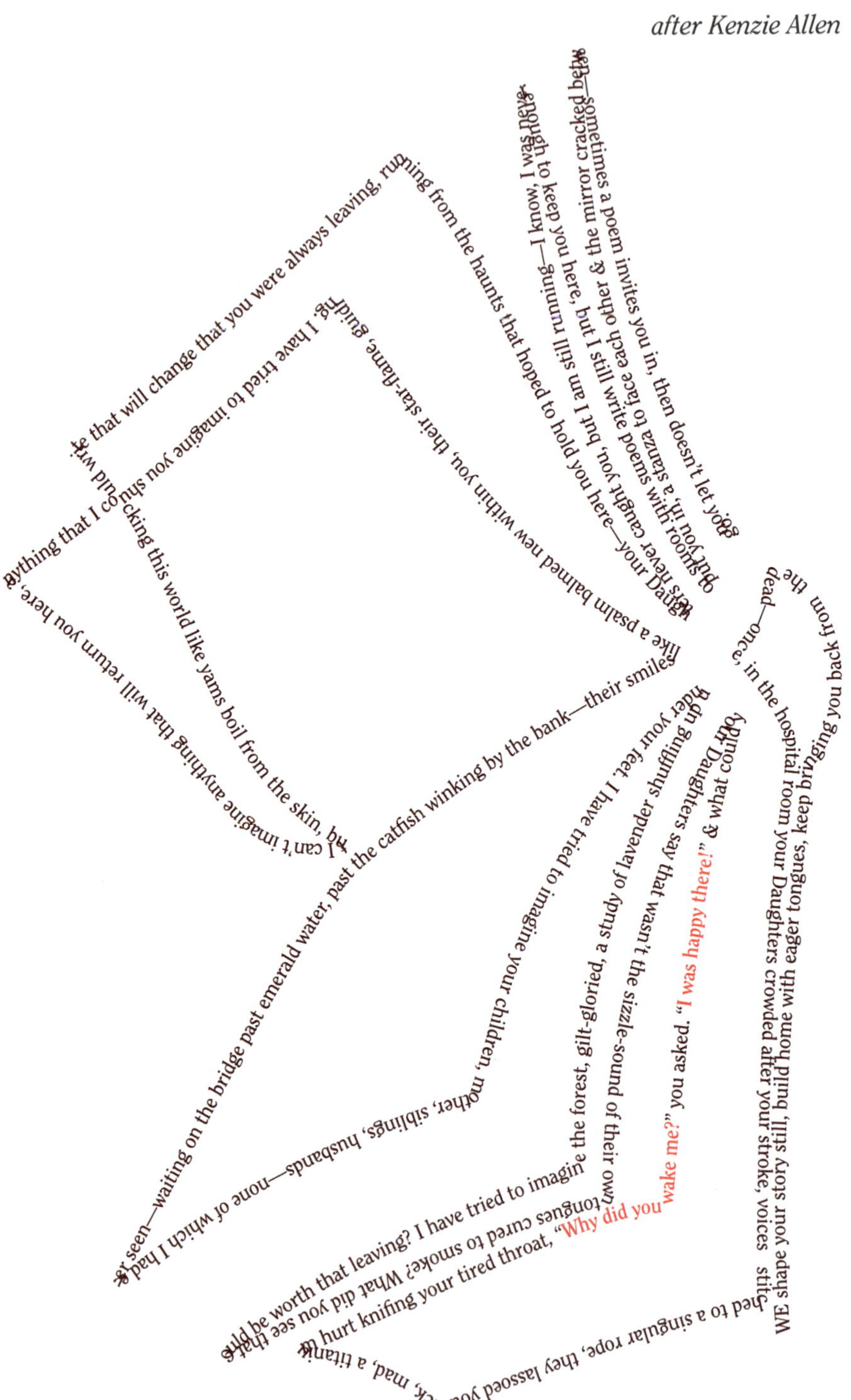

WE shape your story still, build home
with eager tongues, keep bringing you back
from the dead—once, in the hospital room

your Daughters crowded after your stroke,
voices stitched to a singular rope, they lassoed
you back, mad, a titanium hurt knifing

your tired throat, "Why did you wake me?"
you asked. "I was happy there!"
& the Daughters responded

with the sizzle-sound of their own tongues
cured to smoke. What did you see
that could be worth that leaving? I have tried to imagine

the forest, gilt-gloried, a study of lavender
shuffling up under your feet. I have tried to imagine
your children, mother, siblings, husbands—

none of which I had ever seen—waiting
on the bridge past emerald water,
past the catfish winking by the bank—

their smiles like a psalm balmed new
within you, their star-flame, guiding.
I have tried to imagine you shucking this world

like yams boil from the skin, but I can't imagine
anything that will return you here,
anything that I could write that will change that

you were always leaving, running from
the haunts that hoped to hold you here—your Daughters
never caught you, but I am still running

—I know, I was never enough
to keep you here, but I still write poems
with rooms to put you in, a stanza

to face each other &
the mirror cracked between—sometimes
a poem invites you in, then doesn't let you go.

THE BUFORD HIGHWAY FARMERS MARKET

THE night you died, I sat in the dark outside my closet looking to where the jacket hung, waiting for sadness to talon itself from my throat.

2 That leopard-print jacket you bought but didn't fit, so you made me promise to wear it, which I did—promise—flipping my fingers over the stiff denim, brown & bronze, the dark spots flecked along the arms.

3 I loved it but didn't
wear it in your lifetime.
I couldn't keep my promise

4 till my early twenties—after my sister asked me to take her to a rock concert, so we went decked in eighties Madonna-chic, side ponies, mesh dresses, & cheap boots—& for the first time, I put on the leopard-print jacket—loved how it bridged the now with what was

5 around us—an emo crowd crashing against our dinghy of joy, sweat licking our brows, but no matter how hot I collared, I wouldn't shed that jacket—wanted, maybe, to take you to the melodies you used to know

6 on Thursdays—to the Buford Highway Farmers Market, where the bread aisle wrapped the horizon—tender clouds of challah, kaiser, & croissants—rambutan, & rhubarb pies, a seafood market—wet with a salt-brine stink—but you dressed for it anyway—low pumps, plaid pleats, pearl earrings silky as molars.

7 My cousins & I—child-hollers wailing between the rows. But you posed perfect, unbothered, pushed the buggy slow, & when the fish man saw you go, he sang your sugared name like a soprano—*Heyyy, Miss Alice*—then you'd duet, laughter bubbling up somewhere among the snapper, the whole cold aisle whizzing a tune.

PIG FEET & BLACK-EYED PEAS

HER knife knuckles   between the toes,   splits
an onion, phosphorescent   sliver of the moon,
peas twice soaked   & boiling, bay leaf   & bell
pepper,   bouillon, salt, the whole house
smellin' like down-home   grease & garlic,
procreant stank on the stove,   Alice knows
hunger, its costumes—tight-belly-tweed-
  hunger,   orgasms in organza, even
the cotton-mouthed hunger of home.
Beans blink in the pot. Trotters split their sinew, sigh.
Upstairs, her husband's brother
duets with Otis,   tries a little tenderness, & a two-step
shuffles down, stirs   the kids from their beds.
She will mother them
    the way she once was mothered: psalms still wet
in her smile, each kiss   a map back—Alice throws
the window open, & heat carries
    the sweet stink to the borough.

WHAT I SHOULDA SAID WHEN YOU ASKED ME IF I'D GO TO GRANDMA'S FUNERAL

THERE'S a fig tree feathering behind the old brick building at work, & each fall it droops with new fruit, green bulbs purpling like bruises, fresh with flushed meat, seeds pink as flagging tongues, & there's a cove cratered beneath the broad leaves large enough to sit in, to reach for every wine-dark drop, eat, cream it against my teeth

& isn't it divine to hide behind fig leaves?

or that for each fruit to bloom, a mother dies—a wasp slipping into the fig's snug end, wings clipped in entry, antennae ripped from the stalk—blinded by a need to breed, which is not a metaphor, but an insect giving body for brood—because love is a force greater than grief

& we weren't meant to mother

because martyrdom, that supposed mechanism of mothering, won't tick in me, but I know love, found it in the joyful tunes of my own breath, in my hands clapping verbs to thunder, in my thigh's singular notes, & maybe if you'd listen, you'd hear it as my grandmother heard it, in her last pulse, that thrum not swan song but a mulch-womb buzzing to fruit.

IN YOUR NEXT LIFE

I wish you barefoot in a grass field as beetles scuttle under the sun-splintered
trunk of a pawpaw tree I wish you autumn after the leaves blush

into red dregs & the mulch beneath your feet feeds the night-marrow
of the roots see how her branches sway sugar-heavy in her sovereign

green & I wish you'd reach eat split the jade skin w/ your thumbs juices kneeling
into knuckle-valleys leaky custard coursing errant lines

along your arm I wish you sweetness laugh-lined
as a testament to peace I wish you standing under stream-babble splintering

over smooth stones water clean enough to lift your skirt & kneel
near the shoreline drink I wish you buoyant brown hips a blush

brushed on the river's slate face I wish you sovereignty
beneath the streetlight's bow incandescent gold glittering back toward the marrows

of home—I wish you a momma heavy-handed who can mark rows
of tender scalp with tight plaits boho-boxed- goddess braids outlined

on the sore edge of sleep— let beauty be the only pain sovereign
over you & may you never bruise nor break never cast nor splint

though I wish you shouting w/ a windmill tongue throat blushing
peony pink I wish you a small church w/ good folk kneeling

at the altar of your heart & I wish you good tunes good weed & good knees
I wish you late nights soft shoes sneaking through marrowed

midnight tryna catch a ride w/ somebody who makes you blush
one last-minute day trip to the ocean just to lounge in the watery line

stitching seas   & when a dolphin dashes   the horizon to splinters
of multicolored light   may you learn then your reign

is arithmetic   is counting your living—as unyielding   as the sovereignty
of stars I wish you   Sunday feasts: pinto beans   collard greens kneeling

beneath the chef knife   whole rack of baby back   so tender it splinter
from the bone I wish you kin   —even if you do not share the marrow

of a matrilineal line—
to grub beside   in the garden by the gardenia   joy coraling a blush

over the setting skyline   I wish you empty highways   windows down—bluish
hum of a bassline pooling in the wells   I wish you no mock sovereign

sirened in your rearview   I wish you communion   may you align
your mouth to whatever   salted body you choose   to kneel

& drink beside   & when you cry   let your tears leach from our marrow
every harm that has tried & failed to splinter us

REVELATIONS

AN ADDENDUM FROM THE SAVIOR

I will not martyr, though when I close
my eyes, I see myself like salmon
caught in a bear's jaws, gasping in another
twilight's drool—I am really here, peering
through the gossamer-veiled visions of my too-
soon death to tell you

2 that I matter most when my
breath rattles through these pages, that no part
of me is worth more than the *they* who came
before—that our cafés, parks, museums, &
gardens: all of 'em fertilized with bone.

3 This earth been force-fed kin
till my blood wouldn't bloom a tree—

4 let alone a house somewhere
where the bass from passing cars skips
like children in the streets . . .

5 & was there ever a martyr who
wanted to be? GOD's own destined to die, but
before that, Jesus in the writer's room, pitching
the lance that would one day pierce his side?

6 If this addendum could be
anything but a tombstone. If you could see in
me nebulas, star clusters reaching their golden
fingers into teeming ink—

7 If you could see in me
language. I write & our stomachs churn their
suns—

8 Once, a son named Emmett
had his face cracked into many mirrors &
millions stopped to see themselves.

9 I do not want to be an altar.
I do not want to be a candle abreast with flame.

10 I do not want to pick prayers
from the space between my ears, to be saint,
which means I've given everything
                                    but you still want more.

THE POET RETURNS TO THE BLUE

I sculpt the brush back, hope to find you in these hills,
walk barefoot as the switchgrass kisses my heels—

I want the mountain to mother me. For each tree to crane its birch
neck & belch a song. I want to be weathered by green,

maple leaves scratching summer against the window
of my chest. I want to find you,

welcoming, in the water-crested stone. I want to forget
the still pond's sorrow, the susans black-eyed & beaten

by sun, that a motor moans in the distance, the looped road
below snaking like smoke. I want to thank you

for each underhanded Mercy that led us here,
that your prayers have planted a purple field of spiderwort

shimmying in the breeze, & it is because of you
that I have come here, the two of us, finally ready for home.

WE MUST BREAK

or the Poet Fights Herself About Her Smallness

"I learned young to be the smallest bullseye." —torrin a. greathouse

my hips root like wild hogs
against my dress   i buckle
a quiet belt around them—this holding back
a harness meant to tether me
            to the rash-mashed belly of the world

& i was raised in the way of field mice, low
nose scrounging against
          any sound shuffled up
                    in the mud   & i feel safest
          rising like smoke   i hope

to make in me a door
that only i can open

                              there is nothing

small about me but i was convinced i had to be smaller

so chiseled all day at my wrists
with a house key
till the welts wet poppy-red

i've always been afraid

bucked against my unkempt tongue
fought myself mostly

                    (stop sobbing. stop sopping globules of snot
                    with your sweatshirt pocket. go shower.
                    shit. brush your teeth—for the love-of-GOD
                    fucking eat—

) the landscape of my childhood
has always been Beyond Pink Barbie

                    (neon god w/ a hot-pink guitar
                                                  a rock bop

till you popped her head from her too-tan neck

—Frankenstein-esque, that parental urge to dismantle
what you say is yours)

how many nights did i cradle that Barbie, coddling under night-
light, her crimped bangs dampened with drool

that i might one day delight in finding
her head fit snug on the tapered bulb—
jaw flexing into gossamered light

(gruesome, but we loved how she cast
our whole room peach hues

& went to sleep mesmerized by her eyes
turned headlights)

was it reckless

if i didn't know
fire needs only one small fumbling

& my parents—

(still asleep,
still unaware of the promised flame
coaxing in their kids' room)   thank GOD i learned
that fear is friend to silence
so hid the evidence, prayed smoke
could dissipate by morning

learned, even, to tuck my singed finger
behind another when i grabbed a glass
to drink, to shrink

to sleep in the dark

that i would rather sleep in the dark

than admit

(stop sobbing. stop sopping—)

my family left me
a generation of   breaking

so i must break
(everything they've given us)

REMEMORY

WHEN Alice moved to New York, she stopped telling stories,
but sometimes could catch snatches of old haints porchside,
whispers tangled in the bottles bluing the yard.

2 She'd pretend not to notice how much of home is held in the mouth
here. GOD puts a pebble on the tongue, & Alice learns to *coffee* & *cloth*
but still packs hominy for lunch on her break at White Castle.

3 A regular asks her to stir her finger in his coffee, & she will
hear in him bluegrass & a murder of crows,
hunger's sickle sinking deep

4 & the past haunts, but what's the word
for when it feeds on future, birds plucking days
like muscats from the vine,

5 & Alice knew the stories, Black folks torn apart
like fruit, but that was there, & here, each day, she'd patch
her wounds, pretend home didn't whistle through her chest.

6 She lets him[1] in.

---

1 they find you face down in a wheat field, days after your heart mined a cavern in your chest. to monster is to ignore the emptiness / you made / to take Alice's memories, shove them in a water-logged box in summer: time-chewed / photos of her girls posed under a hydrant's song, Betamax birthdays, her mother's ring gilded in dust—all gone / the bruises, like an orchid wilted / on her cheek / mercy / is my grandmother's bones / jaw cracked & sealed twice strong / you whipped a ballad of breaking in her blood / & if I listened, I could have heard it / a soundtrack sundered in the roux between my legs / but I am loud & legacy / is for the living / & Last Man, I admit / I have delighted in that open field / where the flies shuffled a two-step / where the sun went about its stroll / so unbothered / that this is what I make of you / a footnote, a stutter in a glebe of grain

CANDIED YAMS

or What to Do When Another Man Hits You

INGREDIENTS

4 swole sweet potatoes
3/4ths cup of sugar (white & brown)
1 smashed orange (just the juice)
a splash of Crown
lemon zest
cinnamon & spice
half lb butter (split in pats)
stove with the gas turned high

DIRECTIONS

1. Swamp the potatoes
in cold water, cut them
top to tail, then roast
till honeyed spit dribbles

down the face of it.
Note: there are over four hundred varieties
of sweet potato, many parented
from poor soil, a wealth of tubers

colored cream, or custard, some bruised
through an open sore night—

2. Knife the earth-roots, then skin,
scoop, splatter the soft guts
into a pot, just hot.

Skitter the sugar. Ash the spice.
Delight in suet's sonnet—the butter
skimmed to a scab—*stir*

until the spoon smacks like a backhand—his cracked knuckles crashing—
Crush the citrus, the orange seeds

scattering like teeth—then grate
the lemon, pitch the gas high enough
to hear heat's holler
& while it roils inside you—the love

you have for him still—scrape
the sugar from the spoon, note
how much it tastes like resentment—
the sweet seething your heat has made.

Let it stew. Let it smolder.
Let the copper pot burn.

TO THE PEOPLE IN HELL WHO WANT ICE WATER

WE heard about you as girls, Sis & I,
blustering our dusty & sun-buttered
butts through the front door begging

for popsicles, *real popsicles*, none of that
fifty-cent "twin pop" shit—forced to share
our cherry takeaways—no, we wanted

PowerPuffs, SpongeBobs, ice cream bars
rough-buffed with bubble gum eyes, & we whined,
brass notes clattering our throats,

till Mama—grave as an obituary—slid two quarters
into my palm & reminded us of you—yes, you—
warden of the prison of money, ricochet

of a police siren, the hand raising the hand
of the man with the gun. There's not a hell
hot enough to keep you in. Everywhere,

there's a family being rooted out of their home,
a school being rebuilt into columns of smoke,
a Black girl being murdered for being. We are burning,

& America sweats beneath her torch. & like you,
I will solve everything with violence.
I will rip through bellied earth, claw past silt &

silicate, mantle & core. I am not afraid to burn—
I have been whittled to the wick already.
& I will get my lick back, crack the Earth open,

let the oceans empty her seas
into billowing steam. Let the rivers rain down like fists.
Let us see how much you can hold.

Tilt your head back. Drink, & drink, & drink
till your bodies burst open. I want to see
the human beat of your heart.

THE SOW SPEAKS TO NOAH

what should I think of this—Mercy
in a near month languishing
on a boat gone nowhere?

2 The tusk & musk of livestock,
gassy camels, chickens flicking
wet flecks of shit, giraffes & they long-necks
forever knockin' somebody flat on they asses—

3 never mind the sheep bleatin' all night,
& that somebody stay watchin' me
piss, eat, & sleep, remindin' me
that I'm the *voice of a generation*—

4 As if that should make me humble.
As if that might make me forget
that the only sky you've given me is a puddle
snagged on the sharp edge of candlelight.

5 It can't be a journey that takes you from home
& never gives you back—

6 Is it a gift that I've survived
to send my kids to slaughter? Better home
is the mouth of their mother.

7 Yes, I will eat my children
before I let their buttocks butter into fatback—
better to boar, gore through the neck's soft meat.

8 & this ain't the last flood, Noah.
Your generations drown my kin
in white noise daily.

9 But did you know a pig can swim
for miles if it gotta? & I'll turn my whole ass out
to open ocean, kick a tremolo
of waves behind—

my whole brood finna wash this planet.

10 O Maidens
of mud,
when the water done
makin' slop
of this earth,
we'll root
in raw dung,
kick wherever
our pink hooves please,
outnumber
the men
who've penned us
here—feed
till our bellies bulge
into boulders—be
too large
for any hook
to hold us.

I CAN'T WRITE ABOUT THE OCEAN WITHOUT IT BEING ABOUT SLAVERY

but what if I want to fuck the ocean? How do we scholar
circum-Atlantic trade in my desire to dip my oyster-moist
on the saline face of Earth? I'm saying I want to straddle
the sea with both hips slapping like rafts, unshackle
from kelp's clasp wrapping my legs, hell, to dive
without needing to net bones from the seafloor,
& sure, maybe this *is* a queer poem, maybe the ocean is
Mami Wata & I want to tongue her trenches or hold
her swells in my palm's small shell, maybe I want to stew
in the primordial brew from which life oozes, but do not
read me from the sea slick with afterbirth. This isn't baptism
or beast, not communion nor kink, & do not think of ships
on the horizon, ghosts in their sails. Instead, a cast
of blue crab scuttling the seabed, or seagrass licking worship
from my feet, or the California sheephead, a carnivorous
species of fish who ain't afraid to flip a Black
urchin on its back, & see, we both know what I did
there, made metaphor dangerous & recklessly
misfit, & this the thicket of trying to unbramble me
into a conceptual sea—see, this poem is about my wish
to pound waves in my wet wonder, it's ass & ashy knees,
my black body literal, & literate—& mine, anywhere.

ACTS OF SUBMISSION

1 Timothy 2:11–15

YOU tell me to submit / so I submit / to fish & grits / to the goodwill of well-timed rain / to sleep-heavy evenings / fan spittin' / one leg peeped beneath the quilt / to July & its night-hot breath / sun-dazzle & singe / that I might spend it eating / heat & heaping bowls of chili—

what nonsense / I am given to—hot pink / dangly earrings / peppermint tea // I submit to the familiarity / of my body: biceps / flapping & clapping like wings / I rise / & submit, next, to poetry / who has wrecked me / like a lover has shown me the pulse of my own pulpy heart / to classroom mumble

to chalk's mean screech / to my students / whose thoughts powder the front of my dress long after a lesson is through // I submit to hard lessons / an ache quaking my gut taught me to listen to rest's sharp plea / & now I submit to daytime naps, nighttime naps, & all the naps between // I submit to writers'

parties, all of us blunt-hazy, stone-eyed, talkin' bout Sappho on a hot porch punctured by flies // I submit to hello / to goodbyes / to the promise that one day the two of us might give in to awkward silence, to good jokes, to picnics beneath the forgotten oaks / downing fistfuls of cut fruit before

the ants suss the sugar out // Grandma, I too have loved a man & made him worship // that one afternoon my partner's hands parted my scalp, adoration in his clippers' shear—tell me, when my hair piled into a perfect nest beside my feet, did you weep? I'll never be the woman / you wanted—

though sometimes I submit to the round of my small dog's stomach, tend its rosy heat in half-hour sittings / & when she squirms under the soft strokes devoted / blooming / I submit to what she stirs in me / this neglected mother need / & maybe it's true, my dog has saved me / & not once did my legs

bear open like a hard smile // I want, only, to de-gender desire / to transgress past the meekness planted in us like overgrown weeds—Grandma, I have freed / the secrets you were too ashamed to keep // which means, I have again submitted / to my unmercied & violent mouth // that I have become / a clitoris

spark / a firework / a girl too loud / with longing / but I deserve each earthly pleasure / before the world flits into hot mist / I will gnaw the flesh from want, slobber on its bones like the man who owns 'em—yes, I am someone's daughter / damn near bald with her hand on her cock.

JELLY DONUT: A FAT ODE FOR UNRULINESS

FRYER-fresh, the yeast dough proofs
balloons in cinnamon heat, batter
buttered, harpooned with jam, a red
wound blistering my thumb—

I want to be this messy. To break the
lines ruling my body, to loosen fat
Black in opulent pools. To axe
my gilded nails through a lumbering

throat. & I crop top, too. Coquette
my blubber, my bust, my profile
is a perfect parabola, my thighs
bread-blow the hemline of my shorts

& I love them, deep brown, oiled
with sun, sweat-sweetened, wet
hips swollen like berries, & when I jezebel
in the marmalade light of a streetlamp

drilling through my window, I strip
skin then, boo hag on the dreamy breath
of a dark room, & when I say I love
the moon I mean I've dreamt

of tongue-punching its gloomy craters,
rock-marked curves globuled with spit,
& this is the love I give, violently
oozing—& everywhere.

DANCE WITH ME, ALICE

KICK it old school—"Square Biz" on the track,
"Rhythm Nation" after that, a two-step, a hip
switch, a wobble & shuffle—shit, we bustin'
like a church choir. DJ, a reverent shepherd,
spotlit on our pelvic bones fluttering to flights

of butterflies, lightning threaded through
our twine—o cacophony, o clatter, o thrill
trilled in our jaws, o skull's skedaddle &
synapse-clap, o menagerie of lap-slapped
moves, o groove, & glory be to my sistahs'

wigs, slack-jawed, hung on by bobby pins
& prayer—o hair, o waking star of heat,
o feet, & heels, o red-soled Christians
peeled & scrapped at the table, o dress
wetted with sweat & must, loin & touch,

o wallflower, wisteria, o morning glory
liquored in light—Alice, take my hand.
What's a dance if not gratitude
between two bodies? Grandma, I've lived
because of you. I've survived as the star

dazzling like a diamond at your earlobe, so
let's bop. Let's pop. Let's boogie-woogie, or
mbuki-mvuki—which means we're naked
as the day we burst blood-wailing from
a tequila-soaked heaven. & we stankin'. & we free.

NOTES

The Book of Alice began as a project of resurrection, in which I returned to the only inheritance I have to remember my grandmother by: a time-worn copy of the King James Bible, one among many that she left behind, but which no less held the truth to who Alice was, what she loved, and what kind of poetry she grew up knowing. The collection has since, however, become an invitation into the lives of several Black women forgotten and erased.

Inspired by the women in my family—the best storytellers I know—I wanted to tell *our* story, the legend of us, with the aim of generational care and recovery for my immediate family but also for the Black women across time and space who, through diasporic connection, are inevitably kin to the themes in this book. Because, as Renita J. Weems writes in "Reading *Her Way* through the Struggle: African American Women and the Bible," "for African American (Protestant) women, the Bible has been the *only* book passed down from her ancestors, and it has been presented to her as *the* medium for experiencing and knowing the will of the Christian God." I hoped that by using the King James Bible to write about my grandmother, I could tend against the silences of legacy, archival erasure, and the perceived excess of Black female embodiment that I know and navigate.

The Book of Alice seeks to recenter the oft-nameless Black women necessary to creation, to ask what happens when we focalize on the Black narratives whitewashed from the most canonized text of all time. The collection follows and affirms the existence of my grandmother Alice, from girlhood to womanhood, during her migration north, and our generational return south, to ask what parts of self-making, of legacy, of inheritance can never be silenced.

In "Record of Deaths: Diamond Forde," the epigraph is the first line from hip-hop artist Doechii's Grammy Award–winning album, *Alligator Bites Never Heal*.

GENESIS

"Origin Story: The Father" is based on a family legend in which my great-grandfather, a white man, pretended to be a door-to-door salesman to secretly meet with and sleep with my great-grandmother.

In "Clabber Milk Cornbread," and the other recipe poems throughout the book, I wrestled with the variations for formatting measurements (2 cups flour? 2 cup flour? 2 c flour?). I decided to imitate the measurements in Malinda Russell's *A Domestic Cook Book*, published in 1866 and credited as one of the oldest cookbooks written by a Black woman.

"Bildungsroman with a Line by Frances E. W. Harper" borrows two lines from the closing couplet of Harper's poem "Vashti," published in *Atlanta Offering* in 1895. Before this, Frances E. W. Harper became the first Black woman to publish a short story, in 1859.

"Lot's Wife" is named Ado or Idit (anglicized as Edith) in Jewish biblical exegesis.

In "Courtin'," the phrase "take me like a mother" is adapted from the first line of Vievee Francis's poem, "Beast and Beauty."

EXODUS

"Southern Fried Catfish": My grandmother loved catfish, although my mother stopped eating them for a time because catfish "weren't really fish." She was, of course, abridging a verse from Leviticus 11:9–10, which states that any fish that does not have fins and scales, like catfish, are an "abomination unto you" and should not be eaten. I often wondered what it might feel like to be the fish considered an "abomination."

"Callin' the Hogs": This phrase is a Southern idiom with several variants, used when someone or something is snoring—loudly.

As briefly described in "What to Do with Your Hands While Dancing," The First Born was murdered during the 1980s crack epidemic, with its disproportionate impact on Black, inner-city communities; my mother had a prophetic dream about his dying the day that it happened. The poem is a response to a sonnet in Terrance Hayes's *American Sonnets for My Past and Future Assassin*, in which Hayes writes, "I don't know how to hold myself when I dance. Do you?"

The "U.S. Department of Commerce Bureau of the Census" sonnet is stylized after a census form found in the United States Census Bureau database from 1960.

DAUGHTERS

The phrase "Swimming is not dreaming, is not flight" in "Census of Daughters" is directly lifted from Monica Sok's poem "The Death of Henry Kissinger."

"Sethe Speaks to Hagar" is a conversation between the protagonist from Toni Morrison's *Beloved* and the biblical figure Hagar (although there are connections to Morrison's novel *Song of Solomon*, too). Morrison's work also influenced other poems that appear later in the book, including "Rememory" and "The Sow Speaks to Noah." Finally, the formatting of *Mr* within the poem is a direct reference to Alice Walker's *The Color Purple*.

LAMENTATIONS

"Pineapple-Coconut Cake": At the time my grandmother was born, Black children did not always receive a birth certificate, so my grandmother's birth date was a bit of a mystery; my great-grandmother always said she gave birth on July 4, but the doctors claim it might have been July 2. So each year, we celebrate my grandmother's birthday from July 1 to July 4. Ideally, with her favorite pineapple-coconut cake—a banana-less variant of the Jamaican-born hummingbird cake, which she also loved. While the statement included in the poem is a direct quote from my grandmother, the Lucille Clifton poem she inadvertently riffs upon is "won't you celebrate with me."

The town of Chimney Rock, which exists just west of the lake in the poem "Portrait of My Grandmother as Lake Lure in Winter," suffered catastrophic damage during Hurricane Helene. This is the last poem I wrote before the storm.

"The Right Words" references a moment in which my grandmother overheard me telling my little sister that I hated her. Afterward, she knelt me down in front of her to be prayed over, while she repeatedly rebuked the devil in me.

The design of "What Alice Saw" is inspired by Kenzie Allen's poem "109 Bermuda," originally published in *Poem-a-Day* on November 22, 2022.

REVELATIONS

In "The Poet Returns to the Blue," *the Blue* is a reference to the Blue Ridge Mountains near where my grandmother grew up.

The poem "To the People in Hell Who Want Ice Water" alludes to the idiomatic expression *and people in hell want ice water*, used in response to someone asking for something that they will not likely get.

"The Sow Speaks to Noah" riffs on a line from Aurielle Marie's poem "gxrl gospel ii: when thrown against a sharp white background" from *Gumbo Ya Ya*: "however drowned I am | by white noise."

Mbuki-mvuki in "Dance with Me, Alice" is a word in the Bantu language that means "to take one's clothes off to dance freely."

ACKNOWLEDGMENTS

With gratitude to the editors, staff, and readers of the following publications in which some of these poems, many in earlier versions, appeared:

Academy of American Poets: "Census of Daughters"; "Rememory" (*Poem-a-Day*, August 2, 2022, guest editor Donika Kelly)
Allium: "An Addendum from the Savior"; "To the People in Hell Who Want Ice Water"
ANMLY: "Poem in Which I Should Write About Cain, but I'm Tired of Writing About Death"; "What I Shoulda Said When You Asked Me If I'd Go to Grandma's Funeral"
Bellingham Review: "Callin' the Hogs"; "Southern Fried Catfish"
Between Paradise and Earth: Eve Poems (Orison Books): "Creation Myth"
Birmingham Poetry Review: "The Right Words"; "Womaning"
Boston Review: "Another Damn Body Poem"; "Family Tree"; "Pig Feet & Black-Eyed Peas"
Callaloo: "Collard Greens & Ham Hocks"; "Pineapple-Coconut Cake"; "In Your Next Life"; "Acts of Submission" (Black Appalachia issue, guest editor Crystal Wilkinson); "Courtin'"
Frontier Poetry: "Lot's Wife"
Gulf Stream Magazine: "Candied Yams" (formerly known as "Candied Yams, or How to Monster"); "Fat Gospel"
Hairstreak Butterfly Review: "On the Train to New York"
Honey Literary: "I Can't Write About the Ocean Without It Being About Slavery"; "Jelly Donut: A Fat Ode for Unruliness"
Limp Wrist: "We Must Break"
Obsidian: "Creation Myth: Alice"; "The First Born"
Poetry Magazine: "Clabber Milk Cornbread"; "Origin Story: The Father"; "The Sow Speaks to Noah"
South Carolina Review: "Ars Poetica with Snow Globes"
Southern Cultures: "The Buford Highway Farmers Market"

Many thanks to the institutions that funded and made space for me to accomplish this work—the Poetry Foundation, the Virginia Center for the Creative Arts, the James River Writers Conference, and the Bread Loaf Environmental Writers' Conference—and to my friends, colleagues, mentors, and professors at the University of Alabama, Florida State University, and the University of North Carolina Asheville whose support made this book possible.

My sincerest gratitude to the friends and colleagues who make my survival possible. Thank you to my first readers, the brilliant and insightful Mo Hakala, Rachel Hanson, and Nabila Lovelace. Thank you to Atlanta, who raised me; to Asheville, who embraced me; and to those in my community who supported each other after Helene. Special thanks to those who listened. Thanks to those who have shown themselves to be sincere and loving friends: Saida Agostini, Kendra Allen, Kay Ulanday Barrett, Sandra Beasley, Dionne Irving Bremyer, Dustin Brookshire, Kayleb Rae Candrilli, Cavar, Dorothy Chan, de'Angelo DIA, Tarik Dobbs, Tarfia Faizullah, Nikky Finney, Yolanda Franklin, Alisha Gaines, Mark Galarrita, torrin a. greathouse, Barbara Hamby, Duriel E. Harris, Sean Hill, Leslieann Hobayan, Douglas Kearney, Donika Kelly, Kiese Laymon, Alan Pelaez Lopez, Tariq Luthun, Aurielle Marie, James Davis May, Troy Osaki, Emily Polson (the best editor in the game), Chelsea Rathburn, Patricia Smith, Robert Stilling, Lynne Thompson, Cy Weise, Lisbeth White, and L. Lamar Wilson. Thanks to my students, who constantly reteach me the possibilities of poetry. Finally, thanks to each and every one of you who are so brilliant, so necessary to this work, that you don't even need me to mention you by name.

And last but never least, thank you to my family—my mom and dad, who are a forever fount of wisdom, grace, and guidance. To my sister, Ana, who has proven to me time and again that sisterhood can stir in you a kind of devotion, and that I am lucky for the sister that I have. The *sisters* I have: Chisa Hutchinson, a brilliant dramatist, and her magnanimous husband, Kyle, who have supported my shine and shined themselves in turn. With love and gratitude for Wesley: my Truth, my soulmate, my best reader and most diligent critic—and the most compassionate caretaker I have ever known. To my treasure, Oatmeal. And to the ancestors near and far, especially Alice, without whom this book could not exist. And to my godmothers, godfathers, aunts, uncles, cuzzos, and them—those who saw in me a greatness long before I could praise the greatness in you—thank you, this book is for all of us.

ABOUT THE AUTHOR

Dr. Diamond Forde's debut collection, *Mother Body*, was chosen by Patricia Smith as the winner of the 2019 Saturnalia Poetry Prize. She has received numerous awards and prizes, including the Pink Poetry Prize, the Furious Flower Poetry Prize, and CLA's Margaret Walker Memorial Prize. She is a Callaloo, Tin House, and Ruth Lilly and Dorothy Sargent Rosenberg Fellow whose work has appeared in *Boston Review*, *Massachusetts Review*, *Ninth Letter*, and elsewhere. She serves as the interviews editor for *Honey Literary*. Diamond earned her bachelor's degree in English from the University of West Georgia, an MFA from the University of Alabama, and her PhD in African American poetics and fat studies at Florida State University. She is an assistant professor at North Carolina State University.